SPECTACULAR
SOUPS

Consultant Editor:
Valerie Ferguson

HERMES
HOUSE

Contents

Introduction

There is something special about home-made soup, whether a sophisticated dinner-party first course or a hearty family chowder. The range is immense – delicate and aromatic, rich and creamy, classically simple and elegant or so substantial that you almost need a knife and fork to eat them. Chilled soups are refreshing on a summer's day, while steaming home-made broth is the best kind of "central heating" in winter. These recipes have been inspired by cuisines across the world from Spanish Gazpacho to Moroccan Harira and from Russian Borscht to American Succotash Soup Plate.

The key to delicious soup is good stock. While stock and bouillon cubes are convenient for some dishes, when it comes to soup, there is nothing like stock prepared from fresh ingredients. On the following pages you will find recipes for four stocks, advice on preparing vegetables and a guide to using herbs as garnishes so that your soup looks as good as it tastes.

Whether you are looking for an inexpensive family lunch or an extravagant and luxurious soup to spoil special guests, a summer cooler or a winter warmer, you will find it in *Spectacular Soups*.

Stocks

Good-quality stock is essential for soups and it is worth the effort to prepare it at home. Home-made stock may be frozen successfully for several months.

Fish Stock

INGREDIENTS
1 onion
1 carrot
1 celery stick
any fish bones, skin and
    trimmings available
6 black peppercorns
2 bay leaves
3 fresh parsley sprigs

1 Peel and coarsely slice the onion. Peel and chop the carrot, and scrub and slice the celery.

2 Place the vegetables with all the other ingredients in a large saucepan and add 1.75 litres/3 pints/7½ cups water to cover. Bring the water to the boil, skim the surface and simmer, uncovered, for 20 minutes. Strain. The stock can either be used immediately or stored for up to two days in the fridge and used as required.

Brown Stock

INGREDIENTS
30 ml/2 tbsp vegetable oil
675 g/1½ lb shin of beef untrimmed,
    cut into pieces
1 bouquet garni
2 onions, trimmed and quartered
2 carrots, trimmed and chopped
2 celery sticks, sliced
5 ml/1 tsp black peppercorns
2.5 ml/½ tsp salt

1 Preheat the oven to 220°C/425°F/ Gas 7. Drizzle the vegetable oil over the bottom of a roasting tin and then add the meat. Coat in the oil and bake for 25–30 minutes, or until well browned, turning regularly to ensure even browning.

2 Transfer the meat to a large saucepan, add the remaining ingredients and cover with 3.2 litres/ 5½ pints/14 cups water. Bring to the boil, skim the surface, then partially cover and simmer for 2½–3 hours, or until reduced to 1.75 litres/3 pints/ 7½ cups.

3 Strain the stock and allow to cool; carefully remove the solidified fat on the surface before use. Store for up to four days in the fridge.

Chicken or White Stock

INGREDIENTS
1 onion
4 cloves
1 carrot
2 leeks
2 celery sticks
1 cooked or raw chicken carcass or
   675 g/1½ lb veal bones,
   cut into pieces
1 bouquet garni
8 black peppercorns
2.5 ml/½ tsp salt

1 Peel the onion, cut into quarters and spike each quarter with a clove. Scrub and roughly chop the remaining vegetables. Place the vegetables in a large saucepan with the rest of the ingredients for the stock.

2 Cover with 1.75 litres/3 pints/ 7½ cups water. Bring to the boil, skim the surface and simmer, partially covered, for 2 hours. Strain and allow to cool. When cold, remove the hardened fat before using. Store for up to four days in the fridge.

Vegetable Stock

INGREDIENTS
1 onion
2 carrots
2 large celery sticks
small amounts of any of the following:
   leeks, celeriac, parsnip, turnip,
   cabbage or cauliflower trimmings,
   mushroom peelings
30 ml/2 tbsp vegetable oil
1 bouquet garni
6 black peppercorns

1 Peel and slice the onion. Scrub and roughly chop the carrots, celery and remaining vegetables.

2 Heat the oil in a large pan and fry all the vegetables until soft and lightly browned. Add the remaining ingredients and cover with 1.75 litres/ 3 pints/7½ cups water.

3 Bring the water to the boil, skim the surface, then partially cover and simmer for 1½ hours. Strain the stock and allow to cool. Store the stock in the fridge for up to four days.

Techniques

Chopping Onions

Many dishes use chopped onions as an essential flavouring, and for stir-fried dishes it is important to keep the pieces even.

1 Peel the onion. Cut it in half and set it cut side down on a board. Make lengthways vertical cuts along it, cutting almost but not quite through to the root.

2 Make two horizontal cuts from the stalk end towards the root, but not through it. Cut the onion crossways to form small, even dice.

Skinning & Chopping Tomatoes

It is sometimes recommended that you peel tomatoes before using them.

1 Using a small sharp knife, cut a cross just through the skin at the base of each tomato.

2 Put the tomatoes in a bowl and pour over boiling water. Leave for 20–30 seconds until the skin splits. Drain and transfer to a bowl of cold water to prevent them cooking. Peel off the skin and chop the flesh into even-size pieces.

Garnishes

Fresh herbs are the perfect partners for home-made soups, providing colour, flavour and aroma. They can be used in a huge variety of ways.

Basil
Roughly torn basil leaves are the ideal garnish for tomato and chicken soups.

Carrot Tops
Not strictly herbs, young carrot tops make an attractive garnish for vegetable soups. Chop finely and sprinkle over just before serving.

Chives
These can be prepared in a variety of ways. Snip them into tiny pieces, chop coarsely or slice diagonally for Chinese and Asian soups. They are perfect with any strongly flavoured, creamy soup.

Coriander
A must for Chinese and Indian soups – chop coarsely and sprinkle generously for an unbeatable flavour.

Dill
Snip into fronds with kitchen scissors or chop finely and use to garnish fish soups.

Fennel
Snip or chop the feathery fronds and use for garnishing Mediterranean soups that benefit from the slight aniseed flavour.

Mixed Herbs
All herbs look good with a simple lemon or cucumber slice or twist. Just place a small sprig so that it pokes out from under the slice. Form tiny bunches into a bouquet – take a few herbs, twist off the lower stems and carefully tease the leaves out with a cocktail stick.

Parsley
Parsley goes well with most soups. A small sprig of flat leaf parsley always looks pretty, and finely chopped curly parsley looks lovely sprinkled on the surface.

Sage
The delicate colour and attractive texture of sage leaves complement chilled soups in particular.

Watercress

The deep green of watercress looks wonderful with pale green, creamy soups or with a contrasting colour.

Avocado & Courgette Soup

Chilli and Worcestershire sauce give a spicy kick to this attractive chilled soup – ideal for an *al fresco* summer lunch.

Serves 6

INGREDIENTS
1 litre/1¾ pints/4 cups
    Chicken Stock
450 g/1 lb courgettes, sliced
2 avocados
45 ml/3 tbsp lemon juice
175 ml/6 fl oz/¾ cup
    natural yogurt
10 ml/2 tsp Worcestershire sauce
2.5 ml/½ tsp chilli powder
pinch of sugar
dash of chilli sauce
salt

2 Peel the avocados. Remove and discard the stones. Cut the flesh into chunks and put in a food processor or blender. Add the lemon juice and process until smooth.

1 Bring the chicken stock to the boil in a large saucepan. Add the sliced courgettes and allow the stock to simmer for 10–15 minutes, until the courgettes are soft. Remove from the heat and leave to cool.

3 Using a slotted spoon, transfer the courgettes to the food processor or blender and reserve the stock. Process the courgettes with the avocado purée.

COOK'S TIP: Remember that avocados will discolour if not used immediately after they are peeled.

4 Pour the purée into a bowl. Stir in the reserved chicken stock. Add two-thirds of the yogurt, the Worcestershire sauce, chilli powder, sugar, chilli sauce and salt to taste. Mix well. Cover tightly and chill for 3–4 hours.

5 To serve, ladle into bowls and swirl the remaining yogurt on the surface.

Vichyssoise

Serve this classic French soup garnished with crème fraîche or soured cream and sprinkle with a few snipped fresh chives.

Serves 6–8

INGREDIENTS
450 g/1 lb potatoes (about 3 large), diced
1.5 litres/2½ pints/6¼ cups Chicken Stock
350 g/12 oz/4 medium leeks, trimmed
150 ml/¼ pint/⅔ cup crème fraîche or
    soured cream
salt and freshly ground black pepper
45 ml/3 tbsp snipped fresh chives, to garnish

1 Put the potatoes and stock in a saucepan or flameproof casserole and bring to the boil. Reduce the heat and simmer for 15–20 minutes.

2 Make a slit along the length of each leek and rinse well under cold running water. Slice thinly.

3 When the potatoes are just tender, stir in the leeks. Season to taste with salt and pepper and simmer, stirring occasionally, for 15 minutes.

4 Process the soup in a blender or food processor, in batches if necessary. Stir in most of the cream, cool and then chill. To serve, ladle into chilled bowls and garnish with a swirl of cream and snipped chives.

Almond Soup

Unless you want to spend time pounding the ingredients for this dish by hand, a food processor is essential.

Serves 6

INGREDIENTS
115 g/4 oz fresh white bread
115 g/4 oz/1 cup blanched almonds
2 garlic cloves, sliced
75 ml/5 tbsp olive oil
25 ml/1½ tbsp sherry vinegar
salt and freshly ground black pepper
toasted flaked almonds and
    seedless green and black
    grapes, halved and skinned,
    to garnish

1 Break the bread into a bowl and pour over 150 ml/¼ pint/⅔ cup cold water. Leave for 5 minutes.

2 Finely grind the almonds and garlic in a blender or food processor. Blend in the soaked white bread.

3 Gradually add the oil to form a smooth paste. Add the vinegar then 600 ml/1 pint/2½ cups cold water and process until smooth.

4 Transfer to a bowl and season with salt and pepper, adding a little more water if the soup is very thick. Chill for at least 2–3 hours.

5 To serve, ladle the soup into bowls and scatter with the toasted almonds and skinned grapes.

ato & Sweet Pepper Soup

This recipe was inspired by the Spanish classic gazpacho.

Serves 4

INGREDIENTS
2 red peppers, seeded and quartered
45 ml/3 tbsp olive oil
1 onion, finely chopped
2 garlic cloves, crushed
675 g/1½ lb ripe well-flavoured tomatoes
150 ml/¼ pint/⅔ cup red wine
600 ml/1 pint/2½ cups Chicken Stock
salt and freshly ground black pepper
snipped fresh chives, to garnish

FOR THE CROUTONS
2 slices white bread, crusts removed
60 ml/4 tbsp olive oil

1 Place the pepper quarters skin-side up on a grill rack and cook until the skins have charred. Transfer to a bowl and cover with a plate.

2 Heat the oil in a large pan. Add the onion and garlic and cook until soft. Meanwhile, remove the skin from the peppers and roughly chop them. Cut the tomatoes into chunks.

3 Add the peppers and tomatoes to the pan containing the onion and garlic, cover and cook gently for 10 minutes. Add the red wine and cook for a further 5 minutes, then add the chicken stock and salt and pepper and allow to simmer for 20 minutes.

4 To make the croûtons, cut the bread into cubes. Heat the olive oil in a small frying pan, add the bread cubes and fry until they are golden. Drain on kitchen paper and store in an airtight container until needed.

5 Process the soup in a blender or food processor until smooth. Cool thoroughly before chilling in the fridge for at least 3 hours. When the soup is cold, season to taste with salt and freshly ground black pepper.

6 Serve the soup in bowls, topped with the croûtons and garnished with snipped chives.

Vegetable Soup with Pastis

A combination of fennel, star anise and pastis gives a delicate aniseed flavour to this sophisticated and elegant soup.

Serves 6

INGREDIENTS
175 g/6 oz leeks, thinly sliced
225 g/8 oz fennel, thinly sliced
1 potato, diced
3 pieces of star anise, tied in a
    piece of muslin
300 ml/½ pint/1¼ cups single cream
10 ml/2 tsp pastis
90 ml/6 tbsp double cream or
    crème fraîche
salt and freshly ground black pepper
finely snipped fresh chives, to garnish

3 Stir in the single cream, bring to the boil, taste and adjust the seasoning if necessary.

4 Strain into a bowl, cover and leave until cold. To serve, stir in the pastis, pour into bowls, add a swirl of double cream or a spoonful of crème fraîche and garnish with snipped chives.

COOK'S TIP: To chill the soup quickly, stir in a spoonful of crushed ice.

1 Pour 900 ml/1½ pints/3¾ cups boiling water into a saucepan, add the leek, fennel, potato and star anise and season to taste with salt and pepper. Bring to the boil and simmer for 25 minutes.

2 With a slotted spoon remove the star anise, then process the vegetables until smooth in a blender or food processor and place in a clean pan.

Gazpacho

Gazpacho is a classic Spanish soup. It is popular all over Spain but nowhere more so than in Andalucia, where there are hundreds of variations on the same theme.

Serves 4

INGREDIENTS
1.5 kg/3–3½ lb ripe tomatoes
1 green pepper, seeded and
   roughly chopped
2 garlic cloves, crushed
2 slices white bread,
   crusts removed
60 ml/4 tbsp olive oil
60 ml/4 tbsp tarragon wine vinegar
150 ml/¼ pint/⅔ cup tomato juice
pinch of sugar
salt and freshly ground
   black pepper
ice cubes, to serve

FOR THE GARNISHES
30 ml/2 tbsp sunflower oil
2–3 slices white bread, diced
1 small cucumber, peeled and
   finely diced
1 small onion, finely chopped
1 red pepper, seeded and
   finely diced
1 green pepper, seeded and
   finely diced
2 hard-boiled eggs, chopped

COOK'S TIP: To speed up the chilling process, stand the bowl of soup in another bowl of ice cubes before placing in the fridge.

1 Peel the tomatoes, then quarter them and remove the cores. Place the pepper in a food processor and process for a few seconds. Add the tomatoes, garlic, bread, olive oil and vinegar and process again.

2 Add the tomato juice, sugar, seasoning and a little extra tomato juice or cold water and process. The consistency of the processed mixture should be thick but not too stodgy.

3 Pour the soup into a bowl and chill for at least 2 hours, but no more than 12 hours, otherwise the texture will start to deteriorate.

4 To prepare the bread cubes to use as a garnish, heat the oil in a frying pan and fry them over a moderate heat for 4–5 minutes until golden brown. Drain well on kitchen paper.

5 Place each garnish in a separate small dish or arrange them in rows on a large plate.

6 Just before serving, stir a few ice cubes into the soup and then spoon into serving bowls. Serve with the various garnishes.

Cucumber & Yogurt Soup with Walnuts

A refreshing cold soup, using a classic combination of cucumber and yogurt, typical of Eastern Europe.

Serves 4

INGREDIENTS
1 cucumber
4 garlic cloves
2.5 ml/½ tsp salt
75 g/3 oz/¾ cup walnut pieces
40 g/1½ oz day-old bread, torn into pieces
30 ml/2 tbsp walnut or sunflower oil
400 ml/14 fl oz/1⅔ cups cow's or
    sheep's yogurt
120 ml/4 fl oz/½ cup cold water or
    chilled still mineral water
5–10 ml/1–2 tsp lemon juice

FOR THE GARNISH
40 g/1½ oz/scant ½ cup walnuts,
    coarsely chopped
25 ml/1½ tbsp olive oil
fresh dill sprigs

1 Cut the cucumber into two and peel one half of it. Dice all the cucumber flesh and set aside.

2 Using a large mortar and pestle, crush the garlic and salt together well. Add the walnuts and bread.

> VARIATION: If you prefer your soup smooth, purée it in a food processor or blender before serving.

3 When the mixture is smooth, gradually add the walnut or sunflower oil and combine well.

4 Transfer the mixture to a large bowl and beat in the yogurt and all the diced cucumber.

5 Add the water and lemon juice to taste. Pour the soup into chilled soup bowls to serve. Garnish with the walnuts, a little olive oil drizzled over the nuts and sprigs of fresh dill.

Borscht

This soup was the staple diet of pre-Revolution Russian peasants for hundreds of years and there are many variations.

Serves 6

INGREDIENTS
350 g/12 oz whole, uncooked beetroot
15 ml/1 tbsp sunflower oil
115 g/4 oz streaky bacon, chopped (optional)
1 large onion, chopped
1 large carrot, cut into
   julienne strips
3 celery sticks, thinly sliced
about 225 g/8 oz tomatoes, peeled,
   seeded and sliced
1.5 litres/2½ pints/6¼ cups
   Chicken or Vegetable Stock
about 30 ml/2 tbsp lemon juice or
   wine vinegar
30 ml/2 tbsp chopped dill
115 g/4 oz white cabbage,
   thinly sliced
salt and freshly ground
   black pepper
150 ml/¼ pint/⅔ cup soured cream,
   to serve

2 Heat the oil in a large, heavy-based saucepan and fry the bacon, if using, over a gentle heat for 3–4 minutes. Add the onion, fry for 2–3 minutes and then add the carrot, celery and the prepared strips of beetroot. Cook for 4–5 minutes, stirring frequently, until the oil has been absorbed.

3 Add the tomatoes, stock, lemon juice or wine vinegar and half the dill, and season to taste with salt and pepper. Bring to the boil and simmer for about 30–40 minutes, until the vegetables are tender.

1 Peel the beetroot, thinly slice and then cut the slices into very thin strips.

4 Add the cabbage and simmer for 5 minutes, until tender. Adjust the seasoning and serve sprinkled with the remaining dill and the soured cream.

VARIATIONS: Red cabbage can be used instead of white. Omit the bacon if you prefer, in which case Brown Stock may be substituted for the Chicken Stock.

French Onion Soup

The onions are cooked very slowly to give this soup its rich, brown colour and delicious, sweet onion flavour.

Serves 4

INGREDIENTS
30 ml/2 tbsp olive oil
25 g/1 oz/2 tbsp butter
900 g/2 lb onions, quartered
    and sliced
2 garlic cloves, crushed
5 ml/1 tsp caraway seeds
15 ml/1 tbsp soft light brown sugar
15 ml/1 tbsp balsamic vinegar
10 ml/2 tsp plain flour
1.2 litres/2 pints/5 cups Vegetable Stock
1.5 ml/¼ tsp yeast extract
grated rind and juice of 1 lemon
salt and freshly ground pepper
sliced French bread and grated
    Emmenthal cheese, to serve

1 Heat the oil and butter in a saucepan and add the onions, garlic, caraway seeds and sugar. Cook, covered, over a medium heat, stirring occasionally, for about 20 minutes.

2 Add the vinegar and cook, uncovered, for 10 minutes. Stir in the flour and cook gently for 1 minute.

3 Turn off the heat and gradually blend in the stock, yeast extract and seasoning. Bring to the boil, stirring, and simmer for about 5 minutes.

4 Stir in the lemon rind and 15 ml/ 1 tbsp of the juice. Serve the soup topped with French bread and cheese.

Fresh Pea Soup

If fresh peas are not available, you can use thawed and rinsed frozen peas.

Serves 2–3

INGREDIENTS
small knob of butter
2 or 3 shallots, finely chopped
400 g/14 oz/3 cups shelled fresh peas
  (from about 1.3 kg/3 lb garden peas) or
  thawed frozen peas
475 ml/16 fl oz/2 cups water
45–60 ml/3–4 tbsp whipping cream
salt and freshly ground black pepper
croûtons or crumbled crisp bacon, to garnish

1 Melt the butter in a saucepan. Add the shallots and cook, stirring occasionally, for about 3 minutes.

2 Add the peas and water and season with salt and pepper. Cover and simmer, stirring occasionally, for about 12 minutes for young or frozen peas and up to 18 minutes for large or older peas.

3 Using a slotted spoon, put the peas in a food processor or blender with a little of the cooking liquid and process.

4 Strain the soup into the saucepan, stir in the cream and heat through without boiling. Season and serve, garnished with croûtons or crumbled crisp bacon.

Watercress Soup

Cooking the watercress quickly preserves the rich deep green of the leaves, ensuring that the soup looks as good as it tastes.

Serves 4

INGREDIENTS
15 ml/1 tbsp sunflower oil
15 g/½ oz/1 tbsp butter
1 medium onion,
    finely chopped
1 medium potato, diced
about 175 g/6 oz watercress
400 ml/14 fl oz/1⅔ cups Chicken or
    Vegetable Stock
400 ml/14 fl oz/1⅔ cups milk
lemon juice
salt and freshly ground
    black pepper
soured cream,
    to serve (optional)

2 Strip the watercress leaves from the stalks and roughly chop the stalks with a sharp knife.

3 Add the stock and milk to the pan, stir in the chopped stalks and season with salt and pepper. Bring to the boil and then simmer gently, partially covered, for 10–12 minutes, until the potatoes are tender. Add all but a few of the watercress leaves and simmer for 2 minutes.

4 Process the soup in a food processor or blender, and then pour into a clean saucepan and heat gently with the reserved watercress leaves. Taste when hot, add a little lemon juice and adjust the seasoning.

1 Heat the oil and butter in a large saucepan and fry the onion over a low heat until soft, but not browned. Add the potato, fry gently for 2–3 minutes and then cover and allow to sweat, stirring occasionally, for 5 minutes over a low heat.

COOK'S TIP: Provided you leave out the cream, this is a low-calorie but nutritious soup which, served with crusty bread, makes a delicious and satisfying meal.

5 Pour the soup into warmed soup dishes and swirl in a little soured cream, if using, just before serving.

VARIATION: Try substituting a little fresh orange juice for some of the stock, if you like.

Wild Mushroom Soup

Dried mushrooms have a concentrated flavour and aroma and, although expensive, only a small quantity is required.

Serves 6–8

INGREDIENTS
25 g/1 oz dried wild mushrooms,
    such as morels or porcini
1.5 litres/2½ pints/6¼ cups Chicken or
    Vegetable Stock
25 g/1 oz/2 tbsp butter
2 onions, coarsely chopped
2 garlic cloves, chopped
900 g/2 lb button or other cultivated
    mushrooms, trimmed and sliced
2.5 ml/½ tsp dried thyme
1.5 ml/¼ tsp freshly grated nutmeg
30–45 ml/2–3 tbsp plain flour
120 ml/4 fl oz/½ cup Madeira or dry sherry
120 ml/4 fl oz/½ cup crème fraîche
    or soured cream
salt and freshly ground black pepper
snipped fresh chives, to garnish

2 In a large heavy-based saucepan, melt the butter over a medium heat. Cook the onions for 5–7 minutes, until softened and just golden.

3 Add the garlic and fresh mushrooms and cook for 4–5 minutes, until they soften, then add the seasoning, thyme, nutmeg and flour. Cook for about 3 minutes, stirring, until well blended.

4 Add the Madeira or sherry, the remaining chicken stock, the dried mushrooms and liquid and cook, covered, over a medium heat for 30–40 minutes until the mushrooms are very tender.

1 Rinse the dried mushrooms. Place them in a pan with 250 ml/8 fl oz/ 1 cup of the stock and gradually bring to the boil. Remove from the heat and set aside for 30–40 minutes.

5 Process the soup in batches in a blender or food processor. Strain it back into the saucepan, pressing firmly to force the purée through the sieve. Stir in the crème fraîche or soured cream and sprinkle with the snipped chives just before serving.

COOK'S TIP: Serve the mushroom soup with a little extra crème fraîche or soured cream at room temperature swirled on top, if you like. Add just before sprinkling with the chives.

Carrot & Coriander Soup

Carrots make excellent soups as they purée well and have an earthy flavour which complements the sharper flavours of herbs and spices.

Serves 4–6

INGREDIENTS
450 g/1 lb carrots, preferably young
    and tender
15 ml/1 tbsp sunflower oil
40 g/1½ oz/3 tbsp butter
1 onion, chopped
1 celery stick, sliced, plus 2–3 pale
    leafy celery tops
2 small potatoes, chopped
1 litre/1¾ pints/4 cups
    Chicken or Vegetable Stock
10–15 ml/2–3 tsp ground coriander
15 ml/1 tbsp chopped
    fresh coriander
200 ml/7 fl oz/scant 1 cup milk
salt and freshly ground black pepper

1 Cut the carrots into chunks. Heat the oil and 25 g/1 oz/2 tbsp of the butter in a heavy-based saucepan and fry the onion for 3–4 minutes over a low heat, until it is slightly softened, but not browned.

2 Add the celery stick and potatoes to the pan, cook for a few minutes and then add the carrots. Fry over a low heat, stirring frequently, for 3–4 minutes, and then cover. Reduce the heat even further and sweat for about 10 minutes. Shake the pan or stir occasionally so the vegetables do not stick to the base.

3 Add the stock, bring to the boil and then partially cover and simmer for a further 8–10 minutes, until the carrots and potatoes are tender.

4 Remove 6–8 tiny celery leaves for garnish and finely chop the celery tops. Melt the remaining butter in a small saucepan and fry the ground coriander, stirring constantly, for about 1 minute.

5 Reduce the heat and add the celery tops and fresh coriander and fry for about 1 minute. Set aside. Process the soup in a food processor or blender and pour into a clean saucepan. Stir in the milk, coriander mixture and seasoning. Heat gently, taste and adjust the seasoning. Serve garnished with the reserved celery leaves.

VARIATION: For a more piquant flavour, add a little lemon juice just before serving.

Cream of Spinach Soup

This rich and smooth soup is packed with flavour and, served with crusty bread, would make a light lunch.

Serves 4

INGREDIENTS
500 g/1¼ lb fresh young spinach,
   well washed
1.2 litres/2 pints/5 cups salted water
2 onions, very finely
   chopped or minced
25 g/1 oz/2 tbsp butter
45 ml/3 tbsp plain flour
250 ml/8 fl oz/1 cup double cream
salt and freshly ground black pepper
2 hard-boiled eggs, sliced, and
   2 grilled rindless bacon rashers,
   crumbled, to garnish

1 Remove and discard any coarse stems from the spinach leaves. Bring the salted water to the boil in a large pan. Add the spinach and cook for 5–6 minutes. Strain the spinach and reserve the liquid.

2 Place the strained spinach in a food processor or blender and process to form a purée.

3 Fry the chopped or minced onions in the butter in a large pan until pale golden brown. Remove from the heat and sprinkle in the flour. Return the mixture to the heat and cook for a further 1–2 minutes to cook the flour.

4 Stir the reserved spinach liquid into the onion mixture and, once it is all incorporated, bring it back to the boil.

5 Cook until thick then stir in the spinach purée and double cream. Reheat and adjust the seasoning. Serve the soup in bowls garnished with extra pepper and sliced egg, and sprinkled with the crumbled bacon pieces.

Asparagus Soup with Crab

This luxurious soup would make a superb and impressive first course for a formal dinner party.

Serves 6–8

INGREDIENTS
1.3 kg/3 lb fresh asparagus
25 g/1 oz/2 tbsp butter
1.5 litres/2½ pints/6¼ cups
   Chicken or Vegetable Stock
30 ml/2 tbsp cornflour
120 ml/4 fl oz/½ cup whipping cream
salt and freshly ground
   black pepper
175–200 g/6–7 oz white crab meat,
   to garnish (optional)

1 Trim the woody ends from the bottom of the asparagus spears and cut the spears into 2.5 cm/1 in pieces.

2 Melt the butter in a heavy saucepan or flameproof casserole over a medium high heat. Add the asparagus stalks and cook for 4 minutes, stirring frequently, then add the tips and cook for 2 minutes, until they are bright green, but not browned.

3 Add the stock and bring to the boil over a high heat, skimming off any foam that rises to the surface. Simmer over a medium heat for 3–5 minutes, until the asparagus is tender, yet crisp. Reserve 12–16 of the asparagus tips for garnishing. Season with salt and freshly ground black pepper, cover and continue cooking for about 15–20 minutes, until very tender.

4 Process the soup in a blender or food processor and pass the mixture through the fine blade of a food mill back into the saucepan. Return the soup to the boil over a medium heat.

5 Blend the cornflour in 30–45 ml/ 2–3 tbsp cold water and whisk into the boiling soup to thicken, then stir in the cream. Adjust the seasoning.

6 To serve, ladle the soup into bowls and top each with a spoonful of the crab meat, if using, and a few of the reserved asparagus tips.

.estrone

This heart-warming Italian vegetable soup is so substantial that it is virtually a meal in itself.

Serves 4

INGREDIENTS
1 large leek, thinly sliced
2 carrots, chopped
1 courgette, thinly sliced
115 g/4 oz green beans, halved
2 celery sticks, thinly sliced
45 ml/3 tbsp olive oil
1.5 litres/2½ pints/6¼ cups Brown or
    Vegetable Stock or water
400 g/14 oz can chopped tomatoes
15 ml/1 tbsp chopped
    fresh basil
5 ml/1 tsp chopped fresh thyme or
    2.5 ml/½ tsp dried thyme
400 g/14 oz can cannellini or
    kidney beans
50 g/2 oz/½ cup small pasta shapes
salt and freshly ground
    black pepper

FOR THE GARNISH
freshly grated Parmesan
    cheese (optional)
chopped fresh parsley

1 Put the leek, carrots, courgette, beans and celery into a large saucepan, together with the olive oil. Heat until the oil is sizzling, then reduce the heat to very low, cover and cook, shaking the pan from time to time to avoid sticking, for 15 minutes.

2 Add the stock or water, chopped tomatoes, basil and thyme and season to taste with salt and freshly ground black pepper. Bring to the boil, cover and allow to simmer over a low heat for about 30 minutes, until the vegetables are tender.

3 Add the cannellini or kidney beans, together with their can juices, and mix thoroughly, being careful not to break up the beans. Add the pasta shapes, bring the mixture back to the boil, reduce the heat and simmer for a further 8–10 minutes, until the pasta is tender, but still firm to the bite.

4 Taste and adjust the seasoning, if necessary, and ladle into warmed soup bowls. Sprinkle with Parmesan, if using, and the chopped parsley, and serve immediately.

COOK'S TIP: Minestrone is also delicious served cold on a hot summer's day. In fact, the flavour improves if it is made a day or two ahead and stored in the fridge. It can also be frozen and reheated.

...ey & Vegetable Soup

This soup comes from the north of Italy and is a thick, nourishing and warming winter dish.

Serves 6–8

INGREDIENTS
225 g/8 oz/1 cup pearl barley
2 litres/3½ pints/8 cups
    Brown Stock or water, or a
    combination of both
45 ml/3 tbsp olive oil
2 carrots, finely chopped
1 large onion, finely chopped
2 celery sticks,
    finely chopped
1 leek, thinly sliced
1 large potato, finely chopped
115 g/4 oz/½ cup diced ham
1 bay leaf
45 ml/3 tbsp chopped
    fresh parsley
1 small fresh rosemary sprig
salt and freshly ground
    black pepper
freshly grated Parmesan cheese,
    to serve (optional)

1 Pick over the barley, and discard any stones or other particles. Wash it in cold water. Put in fresh cold water to soak for at least 3 hours.

COOK'S TIP: Serve this soup with plenty of crusty Italian bread for a simple and satisfying meal.

2 Drain the barley and place in a large saucepan with the stock or water. Bring to the boil, lower the heat and simmer for 1 hour. Skim off any scum that forms on the surface.

3 Stir in the oil, all the vegetables and the ham. Add the bay leaf, chopped fresh parsley and rosemary sprig. If necessary add more water. The ingredients should be covered by at least 2.5 cm/1 in. Simmer for 1–1½ hours, or until the vegetables and barley are very tender.

VARIATION: An excellent vegetarian version of this soup can be made by using vegetable stock instead of meat stock, and omitting the ham.

4 Taste the soup for seasoning, adding salt and freshly ground black pepper as necessary. Serve hot, sprinkled with the grated Parmesan cheese, if desired.

Italian Bean Soup

In Italy, *ribollita* is traditionally served ladled over bread and a rich green vegetable, although you could omit this for a lighter version.

Serves 6–8

INGREDIENTS
45 ml/3 tbsp olive oil
2 onions, chopped
2 carrots, sliced
4 garlic cloves, crushed
2 celery sticks, thinly sliced
1 fennel bulb, trimmed
   and chopped
2 large courgettes, thinly sliced
400 g/14 oz can chopped tomatoes
30 ml/2 tbsp pesto
900 ml/1½ pints/3¾ cups
   Vegetable Stock
400 g/14 oz can haricot or
   borlotti beans, drained
salt and freshly ground
   black pepper

TO FINISH
15 ml/1 tbsp extra virgin olive oil,
   plus extra for drizzling
450 g/1 lb young spinach
6–8 slices white bread
Parmesan cheese shavings

1 Heat the olive oil in a large, heavy-based saucepan. Add the onions, carrots, garlic, celery and fennel and fry over a medium heat, stirring occasionally, for 10 minutes. Add the courgettes and fry, stirring occasionally, for a further 2 minutes.

2 Add the chopped tomatoes, pesto, vegetable stock and haricot or borlotti beans and mix thoroughly. Bring to the boil. Lower the heat, cover and simmer gently for 25–30 minutes, until all the vegetables are completely tender. Season to taste with salt and freshly ground black pepper.

3 To finish, heat the olive oil in a heavy-based frying pan. Add the spinach and fry, stirring frequently to avoid sticking, for 2 minutes or until the spinach has wilted.

4 Place the bread in individual soup bowls and divide the spinach among them. Ladle over the soup and serve immediately, with extra olive oil for drizzling and shavings of Parmesan cheese for sprinkling.

VARIATION: Use other dark greens, such as chard or cabbage instead of the spinach; shred and cook until tender.

41

Butternut Squash Soup

The combination of cream, curry powder and horseradish makes a wonderful topping for this beautiful golden soup.

Serves 6

INGREDIENTS
1 butternut squash
1 cooking apple
25 g/1 oz/2 tbsp butter
1 onion, finely chopped
5–10 ml/1–2 tsp curry powder
900 ml/1½ pints/3¾ cups
   Chicken or Vegetable Stock
5 ml/1 tsp chopped fresh sage,
   plus extra, finely shredded, to garnish
150 ml/¼ pint/⅔ cup
   apple juice
salt and freshly ground
   black pepper

CURRIED HORSERADISH CREAM
60 ml/4 tbsp double cream
10 ml/2 tsp horseradish sauce
2.5 ml/½ tsp curry powder

1 Peel the squash, remove the seeds and chop the flesh. Peel, core and chop the apple.

COOK'S TIP: You might like to try using one of the range of curry pastes widely available in Indian stores and supermarkets. They tend to have a fresher taste than curry powder.

2 Heat the butter in a large saucepan. Add the onion and cook, stirring occasionally, for 5 minutes, until soft. Stir in the curry powder. Cook to bring out the flavour, stirring constantly, for 2 minutes.

3 Add the stock, squash, apple and sage. Bring to the boil, lower the heat, cover and simmer for 20 minutes, until the squash and apple are soft.

4 Meanwhile, make the horseradish cream. Whip the cream in a bowl until stiff, then stir in the horseradish sauce and curry powder. Cover and chill until required.

5 Process the soup in a blender or food processor. Return to the clean pan and add the apple juice, with salt and pepper to taste. Reheat gently, without allowing the soup to boil.

6 Place the soup in individual bowls and garnish with a few shredded sage leaves. Serve immediately with the horseradish cream handed round separately or spooned on top.

Vegetable Soup with Coconut

This is a subtly spiced traditional African soup.

Serves 4

INGREDIENTS
30 ml/2 tbsp butter or margarine
½ red onion, finely chopped
175 g/6 oz each, turnip, sweet potato and
   pumpkin, diced
5 ml/1 tsp dried marjoram
2.5 ml/½ tsp ground ginger
1.5 ml/¼ tsp ground cinnamon
15 ml/1 tbsp chopped spring onion
1 litre/1¾ pint/4 cups Vegetable Stock
30 ml/2 tbsp flaked almonds
1 fresh chilli, seeded and chopped
5 ml/1 tsp sugar
25 g/1 oz creamed coconut
salt and freshly ground black pepper
chopped coriander, to garnish

1 Melt the butter or margarine in a large non-stick saucepan. Fry the onion for 4–5 minutes. Add the diced vegetables and fry for 3–4 minutes.

2 Add the marjoram, ginger, cinnamon, spring onion, salt and pepper. Fry over a low heat, stirring frequently, for about 10 minutes.

3 Add the stock, almonds, chilli and sugar and stir to mix, then cover and simmer gently for 10–15 minutes, until the vegetables are just tender.

4 Grate the coconut into the soup and stir. Sprinkle with coriander, spoon into warmed bowls and serve.

Spicy Peanut Soup

A thick and warming vegetable soup, flavoured with chilli and peanuts.

Serves 6

INGREDIENTS
30 ml/2 tbsp oil
1 large onion, finely chopped
2 garlic cloves, crushed
5 ml/1 tsp mild chilli powder
2 red peppers, seeded and finely chopped
225 g/8 oz carrots, finely chopped
225 g/8 oz potatoes, finely chopped
3 celery sticks, sliced
900 ml/1½ pints/3¾ cups
  Vegetable Stock
90 ml/6 tbsp crunchy peanut butter
115 g/4 oz/⅔ cup sweetcorn
salt and freshly ground black pepper
roughly chopped unsalted roasted peanuts,
  to garnish

1 Heat the oil in a large pan and cook the onion and garlic for about 3 minutes. Add the chilli powder and cook for a further 1 minute.

2 Add the peppers, carrots, potatoes and celery. Stir well, then cook, stirring occasionally, for a further 4 minutes.

3 Stir in the vegetable stock, crunchy peanut butter and sweetcorn and mix until combined.

4 Season well. Bring to the boil, cover and simmer for 20 minutes, or until all the vegetables are tender. Adjust the seasoning before serving, sprinkled with chopped peanuts.

Bouillabaisse

Perhaps the most famous of all Mediterranean soups, this recipe is a rich and colourful mixture of fish and shellfish.

Serves 4–6

INGREDIENTS
1.5 kg/3–3½ lb mixed fish and raw shellfish, such as red mullet, John Dory, monkfish, red snapper, whiting, large prawns and clams
225 g/8 oz well-flavoured tomatoes
pinch of saffron strands
90 ml/6 tbsp olive oil
1 onion, sliced
1 leek, sliced
1 celery stick, sliced
2 garlic cloves, crushed
1 bouquet garni
1 strip pared orange rind
2.5 ml/½ tsp fennel seeds
15 ml/1 tbsp tomato purée
10 ml/2 tsp Pernod
4–6 thick slices French bread
45 ml/3 tbsp chopped fresh parsley
salt and freshly ground black pepper

1 Remove the heads, tails and fins and put them in a large pan, with 1.2 litres/2 pints/5 cups water. Bring to the boil, and simmer for 15 minutes. Strain, and reserve the stock.

2 Cut the fish into large chunks. Leave the shellfish in their shells. Scald the tomatoes, then drain and refresh in cold water. Peel and roughly chop them. Soak the saffron in 15–30 ml/ 1–2 tbsp hot water.

3 Heat the olive oil in a large pan, add the onion, leek and celery and cook until softened.

4 Add the garlic, bouquet garni, orange rind, fennel seeds and chopped tomatoes to the pan, then stir in the saffron and its soaking water and the reserved fish stock. Season with salt and freshly ground black pepper, then bring to the boil and simmer for 30–40 minutes.

5 Add the shellfish and boil for about 6 minutes. Add the fish and cook the mixture for a further 6–8 minutes, until the fish flakes easily.

6 Using a slotted spoon, transfer the fish to a warmed serving platter. Keep the liquid boiling, to allow the olive oil to emulsify with the broth. Add the tomato purée and Pernod.

7 Check the seasoning. To serve, place a slice of French bread in each soup bowl, pour the broth over the top and serve the fish separately, sprinkled with the fresh parsley.

Sweetcorn & Scallop Chowder

Fresh home-grown sweetcorn is ideal for this chowder, although canned or frozen sweetcorn also works well. This soup makes a perfect lunch dish.

Serves 4–6

INGREDIENTS

2 ears of corn or 200 g/7 oz frozen
  or canned sweetcorn
600 ml/1 pint/2½ cups milk
15 g/½ oz/1 tbsp butter or margarine
1 small leek or onion, chopped
40 g/1½ oz smoked streaky bacon
  finely chopped
1 small garlic clove, crushed
1 small green pepper, seeded and diced
1 celery stick, chopped
1 medium potato, diced
15 ml/1 tbsp plain flour
300 ml/½ pint/1¼ cups Chicken or
  Vegetable Stock
4 scallops
115 g/4 oz cooked fresh mussels
pinch of paprika
150 ml/¼ pint/⅔ cup single cream (optional)
salt and freshly ground black pepper

1 If using fresh corn, slice down the ears of the corn with a sharp knife to remove the kernels.

2 Place half of the kernels in a food processor or blender and process with a little of the milk.

3 Melt the butter or margarine in a large saucepan and gently fry the leek or onion with the bacon and garlic for 4–5 minutes, until the leek is soft but not browned. Add the green pepper, celery and potato and sweat over a gentle heat, stirring frequently, for a further 3–4 minutes.

4 Stir in the flour and cook for about 1–2 minutes, until the mixture is golden and frothy. Gradually stir in the milk and corn mixture, stock, the remaining milk and corn kernels and the seasoning.

5 Bring the mixture to the boil, over a medium heat, then reduce the heat to a gentle simmer and continue to cook the chowder, partially covered, for 15–20 minutes, until all the vegetables are tender.

6 Pull the corals away from the scallops and slice the white flesh into 5 mm/¼ in slices. Stir into the soup, cook for 4 minutes and then stir in the corals, mussels and paprika.

7 Allow the chowder to heat through for a few minutes and then stir in the single cream, if using. Adjust the seasoning to taste and serve immediately.

Clam, Mushroom & Potato Chowder

This superb variation of the classic clam chowder is given additional flavour by incorporating wild mushrooms.

Serves 4

INGREDIENTS

48 medium clams, washed
50 g/2 oz/¼ cup unsalted butter
1 large onion, chopped
1 celery stick, sliced
1 medium carrot, sliced
225 g/8 oz assorted wild mushrooms,
    trimmed and sliced
225 g/8 oz potatoes,
    thickly sliced
1.2 litres/2 pints/5 cups Chicken or
    Vegetable Stock, boiling
1 thyme sprig
45 ml/3 tbsp chopped
    fresh parsley, plus 4
    parsley stalks
salt and freshly ground
    black pepper

1 Place the clams in a large stainless steel pan, put 1 cm/½ in of water in the bottom, cover and steam over a moderate heat for 6–8 minutes.

VARIATION: If clams are not available, the same quantity of mussels may be substituted.

2 When open, drain the clams over a bowl, remove the shells and chop. Strain the juices over and set aside.

3 Add the butter, onion, celery and carrot to the pan and fry until soft, but not coloured. Add the mushrooms and cook for 3–4 minutes until their juices begin to run.

4 Add the potatoes, clams and juices, stock, thyme and parsley stalks. Simmer for 25 minutes, or until the potatoes begin to fall apart. Season, scatter with parsley and serve.

ccan Harira

This is a hearty meat and vegetable soup, eaten during the month of Ramadan, when the Muslim population fasts between sunrise and sunset.

Serves 4

INGREDIENTS
450 g/1 lb well-flavoured tomatoes
225 g/8 oz lamb, cut into 1 cm/½ in pieces
2.5 ml/½ tsp ground turmeric
2.5 ml/½ tsp ground cinnamon
25 g/1 oz/2 tbsp butter
60 ml/4 tbsp chopped fresh coriander
30 ml/2 tbsp chopped fresh parsley
1 onion, chopped
50 g/2 oz/¼ cup split red lentils
75 g/3 oz/½ cup dried chick-peas,
    soaked overnight
4 baby onions or small shallots, peeled
25 g/1 oz/¼ cup soup noodles
salt and freshly ground black pepper

TO GARNISH
chopped fresh coriander
lemon slices
ground cinnamon

1 Plunge the tomatoes into boiling water for 30 seconds, then refresh in cold. Peel, quarter, seed and chop.

2 Put the lamb pieces, turmeric, cinnamon, butter, fresh coriander, parsley and chopped onion into a large pan, and cook over a moderate heat, stirring, for 5 minutes. Add the chopped tomatoes and continue to cook for 10 minutes.

3 Rinse the red lentils under running water and add to the pan with the drained chick-peas and 600 ml/1 pint/ 2½ cups water. Season with salt and freshly ground black pepper. Bring to the boil, cover, and simmer gently for 1½ hours.

4 Add the whole baby onions or shallots and cook for 30 minutes. Add the noodles 5 minutes before the end of the cooking time. Garnish with the fresh coriander, lemon slices and ground cinnamon.

Succotash Soup Plate

This is a North American Indian dish of corn and butter beans that was originally enriched with bear fat.

Serves 4

INGREDIENTS
50 g/2 oz/¼ cup butter
1 large onion, chopped
2 large carrots, cut into
    short batons
900 ml/1½ pints/3¾ cups milk
1 vegetable stock cube
2 medium-sized waxy
    potatoes, diced
1 thyme sprig
225 g/8 oz/1⅓ cups frozen sweetcorn
225 g/8 oz/2 cups frozen butter beans
    or broad beans
30 ml/2 tbsp chopped fresh parsley,
    to garnish

2 Add the milk, stock cube, potatoes, thyme, sweetcorn and butter beans or broad beans and stir to mix. Bring to the boil, lower the heat and simmer gently for about 10 minutes, until the potatoes are tender.

3 Season the soup to taste with salt and pepper, ladle into warm individual soup plates, garnish with the chopped parsley and serve immediately.

1 Melt the butter in a large, heavy-based saucepan. Add the chopped onion and carrot batons and cook over a medium heat, stirring frequently, for 3–4 minutes, until the vegetables are softened, but not coloured.

COOK'S TIP: Frozen sweetcorn and beans provide the best flavour and convenience, although the canned variety may also be used.

Chicken Soup with Vermicelli

This soup is best made the day before and kept in the fridge overnight. The vermicelli (lockshen) are added shortly before serving.

Serves 6–8

INGREDIENTS

3 kg/6½ lb boiling chicken,
    including the giblets,
    but not the liver
1 litre/1¾ pints/4 cups
    cold water
2 onions, halved
2 carrots
5 celery sticks
a handful of fine vermicelli (lockshen),
    about 115 g/4 oz
salt and freshly ground
    black pepper
fresh bread, to serve (optional)

1 Put the chicken into a very large pan with the giblets. Add the water and bring to the boil over high heat. Skim off the white froth that comes to the top and then add the onions, carrots and celery. Season with pepper.

2 When the liquid comes to the boil again, lower the heat, cover and simmer for at least 2 hours, until the chicken is tender. Keep an eye on the water level and add a little more so that the chicken is always covered.

3 Remove the chicken from the pan and take the meat off the bones, reserving it for another use. Put the bones back in the soup and continue cooking for a further 1 hour. There should be at least 1 litre/1¾ pints/ 4 cups of soup.

4 Strain the soup into a large bowl and chill overnight. When it is quite cold it may set to form a jelly and a pale layer of fat will have settled on the top. Carefully remove the fat with a spoon and discard.

5 Bring the soup to the boil again, season to taste and add the vermicelli (lockshen). Boil for about 8 minutes and serve in large bowls, with fresh bread, if using.

COOK'S TIP: Try to find a boiling fowl to use in this recipe. They have much more flavour than roasting birds.

Lamb Meatball Soup with Vegetables

This family recipe is an ideal way to use up leftover vegetables and it makes a filling meal, served with crusty bread.

Serves 4

INGREDIENTS
1 litre/1¾ pints/4 cups Brown Stock
1 onion, finely chopped
2 carrots, thinly sliced
½ celeriac, finely diced
75 g/3 oz/¾ cup frozen peas
50 g/2 oz green beans, cut into
    2.5 cm/1 in pieces
3 tomatoes, seeded and chopped
1 red pepper, seeded and
    finely diced
1 potato, coarsely diced
2 lemons, sliced
salt and freshly ground
    black pepper
crusty bread, to serve

FOR THE MEATBALLS
225 g/8 oz very lean minced lamb
30 ml/2 tbsp chopped
    fresh parsley
40 g/1½ oz/¼ cup short grain rice
plain flour, for coating
salt and freshly ground
    black pepper

1 Put the stock, all of the vegetables, the slices of lemon and a little seasoning in a large pan. Bring to the boil, then reduce the heat and simmer for 15–20 minutes.

2 Meanwhile, to make the meatballs, combine the minced meat, parsley and rice together in a bowl and season well with salt and pepper.

3 Roll the mixture into small balls, roughly the size of walnuts, and toss them in the flour.

4 Drop the meatballs carefully into the soup and simmer gently, stirring occasionally, for 25–30 minutes. Adjust the seasoning to taste and serve the soup in warmed serving bowls, accompanied by crusty bread.

Thai Noodle Soup

A signature dish of the Thai city of Chiang Mai, this delicious noodle soup has Burmese origins.

Serves 4–6

INGREDIENTS
600 ml/1 pint/2½ cups coconut milk
30 ml/2 tbsp red curry paste
5 ml/1 tsp ground turmeric
450 g/1 lb chicken thighs, boned and
   cut into bite-size chunks
600 ml/1 pint/2½ cups
   Chicken Stock
60 ml/4 tbsp fish sauce
15 ml/1 tbsp dark soy sauce
juice of ½–1 lime
450 g/1 lb fresh egg noodles, blanched
   briefly in boiling water
salt and freshly ground black pepper

FOR THE GARNISH
3 spring onions, chopped
4 red chillies, chopped
4 shallots, chopped
60 ml/4 tbsp sliced pickled mustard
   leaves, rinsed
30 ml/2 tbsp fried sliced garlic
coriander leaves
4 fried noodle nests (optional)

1 Place about one-third of the coconut milk in a large saucepan and bring to the boil, stirring often with a wooden spoon until it separates.

2 Add the curry paste and ground turmeric, stir to mix completely and cook until fragrant.

3 Add the chicken and stir-fry for about 2 minutes, ensuring that all the chunks are coated with the paste.

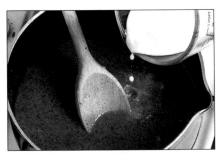

4 Add the remaining coconut milk, chicken stock, fish sauce and soy sauce. Season with salt and pepper to taste. Simmer gently for 7–10 minutes. Remove from the heat and stir in the lime juice.

5 Reheat the noodles in boiling water, drain and divide among individual bowls. Divide the chicken among the bowls and ladle in the hot soup. Top each serving with a few of each of the garnishes.

Beef Chilli Soup

Perfect on a cold winter's day, this spicy soup is warming and filling and takes very little time to prepare.

Serves 4

INGREDIENTS
15 ml/1 tbsp vegetable oil
1 onion, chopped
175 g/6 oz minced beef
2 garlic cloves, chopped
1 red chilli, sliced
25 g/1 oz/¼ cup plain flour
400 g/14 oz can chopped tomatoes
600 ml/1 pint/2½ cups Beef Stock
225 g/8 oz canned
    kidney beans, drained
30 ml/2 tbsp chopped fresh parsley,
    plus extra, to garnish
salt and freshly ground
    black pepper

2 Add the garlic, chilli and flour and cook, stirring constantly, for 1 minute. Add the tomatoes and pour in the stock. Bring the mixture to the boil over a medium heat.

3 Stir in the kidney beans and season to taste with salt and freshly ground black pepper. Lower the heat and simmer for 20 minutes.

VARIATION: For a milder flavour, remove the seeds from the chilli after slicing.

1 Heat the vegetable oil in a large, heavy-based saucepan. Add the onion and minced beef and fry over a medium heat, stirring frequently to break up the meat, for 5 minutes, until brown and sealed.

4 Add the chopped fresh parsley and stir well to mix. Taste and adjust the seasoning, if necessary. Ladle the soup into warmed individual soup bowls and serve immediately, garnished with fresh parsley.

First published in 1999 by Hermes House

© Anness Publishing Limited 1999

Hermes House is an imprint of
Anness Publishing Limited
Hermes House
88-89 Blackfriars Road
London SE1 8HA

ISBN 1 84081 196 X

A CIP catalogue record for this book is available from the British Library

Publisher: Joanna Lorenz
Editor: Valerie Ferguson
Series Designer: Bobbie Colgate Stone
Designer: Andrew Heath
Editorial Reader: Penelope Goodare
Production Controller: Joanna King

Recipes contributed by: Catherine Atkinson, Carla Capalbo, Lesley Chamberlain, Kit Chan, Frances Cleary, Carole
Clements, Trisha Davies, Roz Denny, Sarah Edmonds, Rosamund Grant, Christine Ingram, Judy Jackson, Lesley Mackley,
Norma Miller, Jenny Stacey, Steven Wheeler, Elizabeth Wolf-Cohen.

Photography: William Adams-Lingwood, James Duncan, Ian Garlick, Michelle Garrett, Amanda Heywood, David
Jordan, Patrick McLeavey, Michael Michaels, Thomas Odulate.

1 3 5 7 9 10 8 6 4 2

Notes:
For all recipes, quantities are given in both metric and imperial measures and,
where appropriate, measures are also given in standard cups and spoons.
Follow one set, but not a mixture, because they are
not interchangeable.

Standard spoon and cup measures are level.

1 tsp = 5 ml   1 tbsp = 15 ml

1 cup = 250 ml/8 fl oz

Australian standard tablespoons are 20 ml.
Australian readers should use 3 tsp in place of 1 tbsp for measuring small quantities of gelatine,
cornflour, salt, etc.

Medium eggs are used unless otherwise stated.

Printed and bound in China